What Every
# Parent Should Know
About
# Teen Sex

## The Secret STD Epidemic

*My people are destroyed for lack of knowledge,*

*Because you have rejected knowledge,*

*I also will reject you for being priest for Me,*

*Because you have forgotten the law of your God,*

*I also will forget your children.*

*Hosea 4:6*

Becky Merrifield Ettinger, RN, MSN

XULON
PRESS

# Dedication

*To my parents,*
***Ray and Maxine Merrifield***
*who modeled faith, hope and the love of Christ.*

*To my husband David,*
*who has been my dearest friend and wise counselor.*

*To my children and their spouses,*
*Angie/Jeremy, Sarah/Paul, and Brad/Danielle*
*who are gifts from God.*

*To my granddaughter Baby Bella,*
*who reminds me of how precious life is.*

*To my sister Julie and her husband Rick,*
*who share their family with me.*

*And*

*To my sweet Aunt Helen,*
*who remembers the old days.*

# Acknowledgements

I thank our pastors at Hope Chapel, Paul and Ainsley Harmon for their love, support, and undying love for Jesus and all of our pastors through the years for their wise counsel and commitment to Christ.

I thank every friend and acquaintance who has shared their STD story with me.

I thank my professors at California State University San Bernadino for their encouragement through my Master's Program. Thanks to Shawn-O, Lacey, and Aaron for assisting me with the charts, book cover, & statistics.

And a special thanks to my cousin Robin Minium, who has unselfishly shared her expertise and assisted me in the final draft.

Most of all, I am grateful to every teenager I have met and those who I will meet in the future. God's plans for this next generation are enormous and my goal is to help them realize it, walk in it, and take this world through the power of Christ as healthy individuals. *Thank you, Lord, for sharing Your passion for the youth with me.*

*This book has been in my heart for over twenty years due to God's love for the next generation.*

# About the Author

Becky Ettinger began working in Labor and Delivery in 1980 at Kaiser Permanente Bellflower Medical Center in Bellflower, California following a two year career as a medical-surgical nurse. When a healthy newborn suddenly died due to an undiagnosed STD (sexually transmitted disease), her quest for knowledge of STDs was birthed. Her focus of study included bacterial and viral infections found harmful or deadly to mothers and newborns.

Simultaneously, Nurse Becky began volunteering her time working with teenagers at her church in Westminster, California. Her first speaking engagement was presented to 25 middle and high school students at her Westminster Foursquare Church.

During her Master's Program at California State University San Bernadino, she was encouraged by Dr. Sam Crowell, her *Expository Writing* Professor to publish her persuasive speech paper in 2004. The nursing professors for the next two years continued to encourage publication of her work. This book includes a concise summary of her research regarding adolescents and the Sexually Transmitted Disease Epidemic in America.

Nurse Becky is currently working as an Assistant Professor of Nursing in Southern California teaching Obstetrics, Antepartum, Postpartum, Newborn Nursery, and Women's Health which encompasses Sexually Transmitted Diseases. Becky is a *Clinical Nurse Specialist in Community Health.*

Becky is married, has three adult married children, one granddaughter, and resides with her husband in Huntington Beach, California.

# Contents

# INTRODUCTION

> *"My people are destroyed for lack of knowledge,*
> *because you have rejected knowledge,*
> *I also will reject you from being priest for Me;*
> *because you have forgotten the law of your God,*
> *I also will forget your children."*
> *Hosea 4:6 (NKV)*

During the late 1980s, the Lord seared this scripture into my heart. At that time, I was working as a Labor and Delivery nurse, learning more and more about sexually transmitted diseases (STDs), and was aware that public school education was promoting "Safe Sex." Following each newborn delivery, the physician or midwife would ask the patient what form of birth control they would be using. If a patient replied "condoms" we giggled and joked with them saying, "We'll see you again next year." We knew that condoms were not a good form of birth control due to the fact that condoms may break, come off, or spill their contents. I had used condoms as a newlywed and knew from personal experience how difficult consistent condom use can be in the real world.

During that same decade, I began volunteering my time working with the youth ministry at my church. Our oldest daughter was just entering middle school and the youth pastor needed our help. My love and concern for the next generation of youth was birthed. At that time (1989), I began speaking to teen audiences about the dangers of engaging in premarital sexual relationships.

In preparation for my Master's Program, I was required to take an expository writing course. The final assignment included a persuasive ten page paper on the topic of my choice. The following week, my professor, Dr. Sam Crowell, greeted me and encouraged me to publish my paper. I looked around and asked him if he was talking to me. He reaffirmed that he felt strongly this paper should be published. *The following paragraphs include the bulk of my persuasive speech paper with a few graphs added.*

## Risk-Informed Sex Education

The epidemic rates of STDs, teen pregnancy, and the risk of AIDS have created intense debates over what to do about the sexual activity of adolescents and the associated problems. **No longer is this only a moral issue; it is now a public health issue costing the U.S. $13 billion per year!** Educators, parents, politicians, and health officials agree that we are <u>failing</u> to adequately equip our young people to handle the choices and consequences they face today. [125]

Comprehensive sex education assumed that knowledge acquired at earlier ages would influence behavior. Yet evidence has suggested that younger teenagers, especially, are *unlikely* to act on what they know. After several years of comprehensive sex education we have learned that it has little effect on teenagers' decisions to engage in or postpone sex.[1] In a nationwide survey, 1,245 parents of children in grades K-12 were given exact quotes from Comprehensive Sex Education by Zogby International. This survey was the first poll of its kind.

The results indicate that when parents *hear the truth* about what

such programs promote they soundly reject it. [20,35]

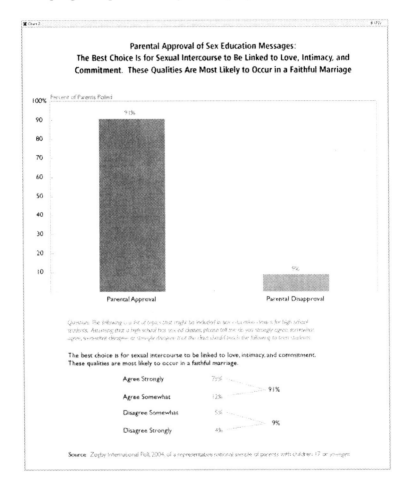

**Parental Approval of Sex Education Messages:
The Best Choice Is for Sexual Intercourse to Be Linked to Love, Intimacy, and
Commitment. These Qualities Are Most Likely to Occur in a Faithful Marriage**

The survey found that 75% of parents *disapproved* of

condom-based sex education curriculum promoted by the CDC.

More than 61% disapproved of "Comprehensive Sex

Education" presented in the classroom, 70% strongly disapprove of their teens getting contraceptives without their approval and 46% disapprove of schools giving teens contraceptives with the approval of "a parent." [20,35] "The message is clear," said psychologist Dr. Bill Maier, "in terms of sex education, parents want their children provided with information consistent with their values and expectations" [20]

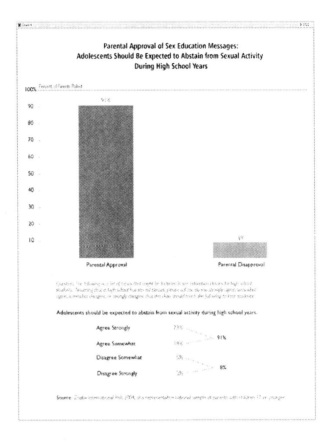

Parental Approval of Sex Education Messages:
Adolescents Should Be Expected to Abstain from Sexual Activity
During High School Years

"We have spent billions of tax dollars promoting the 'safe sex' myth. In return, we continue to see numerous epidemics that plague our nation as well as an alarming erosion of values," said Dr. James Dobson, founder and President of *Focus on the Family.* "Congress should consider the will of parents over the agendas of organizations that profit from teen sex and commit to funding programs that promote abstinence until marriage," Dobson continued. [20]

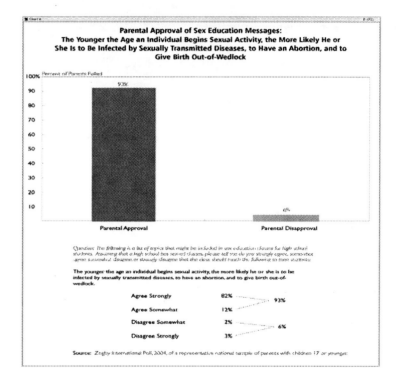

Parental Approval of Sex Education Messages:
The Younger the Age an Individual Begins Sexual Activity, the More Likely He or She Is to Be Infected by Sexually Transmitted Diseases, to Have an Abortion, and to Give Birth Out-of-Wedlock

Source: Zogby International Poll, 2004, of a representative national sample of parents with children 17 or younger.

At the 1987 World Congress of Sexologists, Theresa Crenshaw asked the audience, "If you had the available partner of your dreams and knew the person carried HIV, how many of you would have sex, depending on a condom for your protection?" Of the 800 members present, no one responded. **If the fear of HIV infection for sexologists and sex educators is**

**not reduced with condom use, why would we encourage the children of America to risk their futures?**[1] **HPV,** the human papilloma virus, will infect 50% of sexually active people and some experts say that 80% of people will have HPV by age 50. [32] Health experts estimate that there are more cases of genital HPV infection than of any other STI/STD (sexually transmitted infection/disease) in the United States.

**Chlamydia** infections number *4-5 million* cases per year, one of the most widespread bacterial sexually transmitted infections in the U.S. The **Herpes** virus infects *one out of four women* and *one out of five men* and has no known cure.

## STDs are not equal opportunity diseases

Adolescents have *a higher degree of susceptibility* than do older people.[1] Researchers have estimated that a sexually active 15 year old has a 1 in 8 chance of developing pelvic inflammatory disease (PID), but that by age 24 the chance has decreased to 1 in 80. PID is the most rapidly increasing cause of infertility in the United States and is a primary reason for the 600% increase in tubal pregnancies since 1970. [7]

This major epidemic of STDs has developed during the last 30 years. Today there are over 20 significant STDs with 12 million newly infected persons each year. *It is estimated 1 in 5 Americans is now infected with a viral STD.* This does not include the bacterial diseases which are at very high levels. Sadly, 63% of these infections occur in persons under age 25.

> *Experts recommend delaying sex until marriage as the only sound medical advice that they can offer people in today's environment.* [14]

**Postponing sexual activity until marriage with an uninfected mate is the only way for adolescents to be 100% sure of avoiding pregnancy, STD infection, and their consequences.** Most of them can accomplish this if properly instructed and encouraged. In fact, it was the normal expectation until the "sexual revolution" of the 1960s. Teaching abstinence based sex education is our obligation as healthcare educators.[1]

During the early 80s, HIV was first identified in young homosexual males. Twenty years later approximately 900,000 Americans have been infected with HIV and **more than half a million have died from AIDS.** [14]

With many years of nursing experience, my convictions are strong in informing the next generation of the risks of pre-monogamous sex. Unfortunately, many of our adolescents will not live a full life, have a healthy reproductive life, or have healthy children in their future due to the decisions they are making today.

Perhaps we should re-name our abstinence based sex education "Risk Informed Sex Education." Educating adolescents with the risks of STDs, HIV, and eventual infertility along with positive decision making strategies should be our focus for the future.

At the United Nations' Child Summit in 2002, Uganda's first lady Museveni was characteristically bold in stating, "The young person who is trained to be disciplined will, in the final analysis, survive better than the one who has been instructed to wear a piece of rubber and continue with 'business as usual'. "

# CHAPTER ONE

## Life as a New Graduate RN

As a new graduate R.N. (registered nurse) in the mid 1970s, the medical-surgical unit was my first hospital experience. My duties included caring for patients with a variety of health problems including cancer, heart disease, lung disease, stomach, intestinal problems, etc. On an average night, I had at least one terminally ill patient. Caring for dying patients daily, created emotional attachments between myself and their families. Every time one of my patients died, I would grieve for several days along with the family. I remember several terminal patients and their families to this day.

Part of my duties included preparing the body for the morgue and for the family's final chance to say "Good-bye." After two years of continuous sadness and grieving, I desired a change and found a new love for my work in nursing. I chose a very different type of nursing, "Labor & Delivery," (where the cute little newborn babies were born.)

The hospital I chose contained one of the largest Labor & Delivery Units in Los Angeles County. My unit delivered between 350-450 babies per month, ranking as one of the top ten hospitals in California for the largest number of births per year. In one eight-hour shift we could deliver up to ten babies on a busy night. Due to the size of our hospital we also had a large new Neonatal Intensive Care Unit (NICU). Tiny premature babies were cared for immediately after birth in an NICU. Some of our premature babies weighed only one pound. Amazingly, many of those tiny premature babies survived due to the excellent care they received.

As a Labor & Delivery nurse, I would visit the NICU to check the status of my patients' premature babies. I enjoyed watching the preemies grow in size and strength. Amazingly, these tiny little patients would improve slowly until they were discharged home weighing close to 5 pounds. The NICU staff kept me well informed on the progress of my youngest patients.

Due to our large NICU, many patients were transported to us via ambulance or helicopter. Our unit was considered a High Risk Labor & Delivery Unit which means that many patients due to various underlying problems were *at high risk of losing their babies and possibly their own lives as a result of the pregnancy.*

# CHAPTER TWO

## The Baby That Changed My Life

One evening my assignment included caring for a full-term healthy young woman without any complications or medical problems. After several hours of labor, she delivered a full-term 8 pound baby boy perfectly formed and healthy. After an hour, both mother and son were transferred upstairs to the postpartum unit and the newborn nursery.

Returning to work the following evening, I was *informed that the baby from the previous evening had become very sick during the night and had been transferred into the NICU.* Surprised to hear the news, I called up to the NICU asking what was wrong with the baby. The ward clerk informed me that he had a high fever, was not eating, and very lifeless. The neonatologist had ordered tests to try to identify what germ was attacking the baby. When newborns are sick, blood is drawn and spinal fluid samples are taken. The laboratory examines these samples attempting to discover which germ is causing the infection. If the germ is identified, treatment with antibiotics can often cure the infection.

Each day I called the NICU asking if the lab had discovered the cause of the baby's fever. On Day #5, the lab reported that the baby was infected with the Herpes virus. The doctors agreed the baby had come into contact with the virus during the birth. Most likely, the mother was unaware she was carrying Herpes. As the baby passed through the birth canal, he came into contact with the Herpes virus. On Day 7, **the *baby died... How sad...We were all very sad...***

I began asking questions. "What do you mean the baby died from Herpes?" I was told by the NICU nursing staff that researchers knew Herpes could kill a healthy newborn baby. But this was new information to me! I was shocked and deeply saddened for this couple who were not expecting to lose their healthy baby boy to this virus. This mother had no idea that she was carrying the Herpes virus. The loss of this baby's life changed my own life as a nurse. From that moment on, I began asking lots and lots of questions.

*Following the death of this baby coupled with the news of HIV/AIDS spreading as an STD, I began guest speaking to teen audiences warning them of the dangers of engaging in early sexual activity which could expose them to sexually transmitted diseases (STDs) and their consequences. For the past 16 years, I have continued to speak to young people regarding this topic encouraging abstinence until marriage.*

# CHAPTER THREE

## What's the Big Deal with HERPES?

> *1 out of 4 women (15-49*
> *yrs of age)*
> *and*
> *1 out of 5 men*
> *(15-49 yrs of age) have*
> *Herpes*

The National Institute of Allergy and Infectious Diseases

(NIAID) estimates 1 in 4 women and 1 in 5 men *HAVE*

*HERPES.* That estimation includes all *15-49 year old* men and

women who are sexually active.

You may ask, "Doesn't using CONDOMS stop the

spread of HERPES?" COMDOMS DO <u>NOT</u> provide good

protection due to the fact that the virus sheds off the skin.

*Used with permission from Explosm.net.*

**Have you seen the commercials on TV about Vegas?**

**This comic tells it like it is!**

## Genital Herpes - Initial visits to physicians' offices: United States, 1966-2004

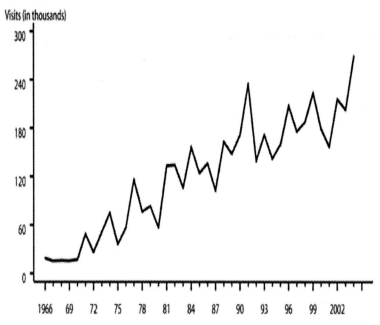

Visits (in thousands)

Note: See Appendix. The relative standard error for these estimates range from 45% to 60%.

SOURCE: National Disease and Therapeutic Index (IMS Health)

*The virus can continue shedding for several days before and after the Herpes lesion erupts. People without symptoms also shed the virus.* We have known condoms provide poor or NO protection for OVER twenty years but how many teenagers have been informed? [17] Sadly, our Comprehensive Sex Ed has not been accurately communicating the complete truth to our teenagers.

As I speak to teens in Southern California, I survey them prior to my speaking. I've discovered that 97.5% of students **do not know that condoms do not prevent the spread of Herpes.** (The virus sheds off the skin. It is a skin-to-skin transfer.) I often ask my audiences, "How many of you have pets like a cat or a dog?" As they respond with a show of raised hands, I convey to them that our pets shed their fur. Just as our pets shed their fur, so does the Herpes virus shed off of the skin prior to, during, and after a lesion appears. Therefore, even if a condom is applied over a lesion, the lesion is shedding and sticking to the hands of the person applying the condom.

The latest CDC guidelines state, "Condoms MAY reduce the risk." Perhaps, this single piece of misleading information could be the leading factor for the Herpes epidemic among American youth.

"Genital herpes is a chronic, life-long viral infection," states the CDC (August 4, 2006). The **symptoms** of Herpes are painful blisters/ulcers which break-out in the genital area lasting from 2-4 weeks during the first outbreak. After the initial break-out, these blisters/ulcers return whenever they choose, lasting approximately 7-10 days.[10] People with Herpes do not know when these blisters are going to break out. For the few days prior to the break-out, the virus sheds off the skin and can spread to other people in close physical contact during that time. Engaging in sex (oral, anal or vaginal) is not necessary to spread the virus. *The data is clear that people without symptoms shed the virus at various times just as those with symptoms shed the virus.* When I speak to students in various meetings I use the analogy of a pet that sheds fur. It helps to give a visual image of shedding. Just touching those areas which are soon to erupt can spread this virus. It is a skin-to-skin transfer of germs due to viral shedding. *Many people who have Herpes have NO symptoms.*[10]

*There is no known cure for Herpes. There are*

*treatments to help reduce the symptoms but there is no known*

*cure.* 10  In the future, if you, YOUR CHILD, or your partner

become pregnant and have a history of Herpes' outbreaks, it is

very important to tell your doctor or midwife. (If you are the

father of the baby, you should inform the doctor or midwife as

well.) When the delivery of the baby is near, you and your

doctor will decide if you will need to have a Cesarean Section

or if a natural delivery IS SAFE.

## Many people who HAVE HERPES Have No Symptoms!!!

There are nearly 1 million internet sites offering

information about Herpes (H). Online "H" communities are

booming.  Many people turn to their computer as a primary

source of information and support following their diagnosis of

Herpes.  One woman with Herpes stated that she found hearing

other people's stories helped heal her emotionally.  People with

Herpes have a strong tendency toward secrecy because of the

stigma that has been attached to it says Dr. VanderPlate, PhD, "Because of that secrecy, there are some people who would never come to a face-to-face Herpes support group," continued Dr. VanderPlate. The internet option helps alleviate the fears of meeting people face-to-face and allows them to receive emotional and ongoing support if they need it.

**Nursing Experience**

Many Cesarean Section deliveries are performed due to pregnant women having a history of Herpes. With every surgery there are risks. Even though the baby is delivered by cesarean section there is still a risk that the baby can contract Herpes.

*At a recent conference, one woman with a history of Herpes spoke to me privately. She explained that she and her husband have Herpes. Prior to every break-out, she and her husband experience severe muscle pain on one side of their body lasting three long days. This woman confided that the three days of severe muscle pain is worse than the actual*

*breakout of Herpes lesions.*

**Abstinence is the only 100% method of preventing transmission of Herpes. Because this virus sheds off of the skin abstaining from all forms of sex is a must!**

Many babies are born via Cesarean Sections due to Mothers having Herpes.

<u>Make sure you are tested for Herpes when pregnant.</u>

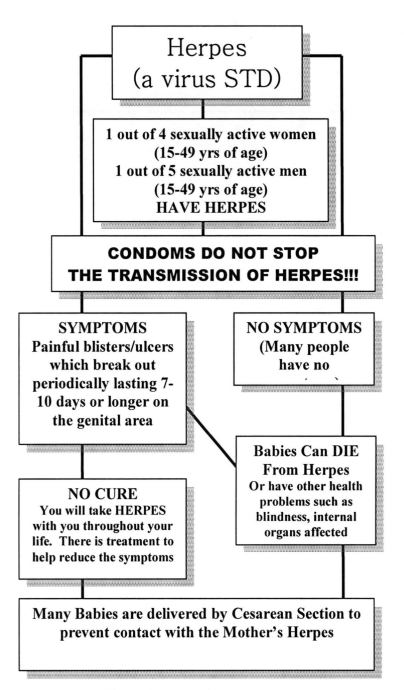

# Herpes
## (a virus STD)

1 out of 4 sexually active women
(15-49 yrs of age)
1 out of 5 sexually active men
(15-49 yrs of age)
HAVE HERPES

**CONDOMS DO NOT STOP
THE TRANSMISSION OF HERPES!!!**

SYMPTOMS
Painful blisters/ulcers
which break out
periodically lasting 7-
10 days or longer on
the genital area

NO SYMPTOMS
(Many people
have no

NO CURE
You will take HERPES
with you throughout your
life. There is treatment to
help reduce the symptoms

Babies Can DIE
From Herpes
Or have other health
problems such as
blindness, internal
organs affected

Many Babies are delivered by Cesarean Section to
prevent contact with the Mother's Herpes

# CHAPTER FOUR

## CHLAMYDIA

*1 out of 8 sexually active people (15-49 yrs of age) have Chlamydia; 85% of females do NOT have symptoms 50% of males do NOT have symptoms*

Chlamydia remains the <u>most commonly reported</u>

<u>infectious disease</u> in the U.S. (4-5 million cases). Experts

estimate that 1 in 8 people in America have Chlamydia.

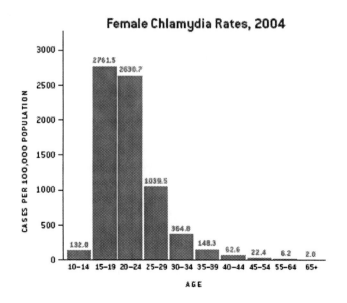

**Female Chlamydia Rates, 2004**

*Source: Trends in Reportable STDs in the United States 2004, CDC*

**Unfortunately, 85% of women do NOT know they have it and 50% of men do NOT know they have it.** Commonly, no symptoms exist at all leading to PID in women (pelvic inflammatory disease) and potential infertility in men and women. Every year more than *100,000 women become infertile* because of PID and more than 150 women die from PID or its complications every year.[7, 17] Like other STDs, Chlamydia can also facilitate the transmission of HIV.[14] Chlamydia is a bacterial infection easily cured with antibiotics. If left *untreated,* however, Chlamydia can cause pelvic inflammatory disease (PID), ectopic pregnancy (pregnancy develops in the fallopian tube), and *infertility* (the inability to have your own babies).

**In women,** the infection can extend from the cervix to the fallopian tubes causing infertility. [7,17]

**In men,** *Chlamydia appears to cause one third to one half of all urethritis (infection of the urethra). The* *infection can extend from the urethra to the epididymus causing male infertility.* [7,17]

**Currently in America, 1 in 4 couples cannot have their** own babies. Of those couples, 60 % are women and 40% are men. To assist with this problem, they must consult an infertility doctor to become pregnant. Infertility procedures, such as *in vitro fertilization* (IVF), range from $6,400 to $11,900 per attempt depending on the patient's age and procedures requested. [13]

> # 1 in 4 couples in the U.S.
> ## cannot have babies.

Chlamydia **symptoms** include an abnormal discharge from the genital organs (vagina or penis). Chlamydia can be treated and cured with antibiotics. Infected partners must be treated at the same time for the infection to be cured. If this infection is not cured, it can be passed on to the newborn baby causing eye infections or pneumonia. [27] Researchers feel that condoms may help reduce the risk of Chlamydia transmission.

# THE ONLY 100% WAY TO PREVENT TRANSMISSION OF CHLAMYDIA IS ABSTINENCE.

## Nursing Experience

Years ago, I admitted a 22 year old woman into my Medical-Surgical Unit. Her admitting diagnosis was PID. Her fever was 104.8 degrees and she was experiencing intense abdominal pain. For several days she received large quantities of intravenous antibiotics. Slowly, she improved and was discharged home. Years later, I realized that infection most likely ruined her reproductive organs causing infertility (inability to become pregnant and have babies). (In some areas of the United States, *young women die from PID.*)

The epididymus tube can become scarred from Chlamydia causing the tube to be blocked. This means a man cannot cause a woman to become pregnant due to the sperm's inability to pass through the reproductive male organs.

Currently in America, *one in four couples* cannot conceive and become pregnant on their own due to the scarring and damage to their respective tubes. Of those infertile couples, 60 percent are women and 40 percent are male.

## Chlamydia causes Lifelong Reactive Arthritis (Reiter's Syndrome)

**Reactive Arthritis** (Reiter's Syndrome) is most often caused by Chlamydia and affects all of the joints of the human body. It is more common in men than women. Reactive arthritis may be self limiting, frequently recurring or develop continually. Most patients have severe symptoms lasting a few weeks to six months. Approximately, 15-50 percent of cases have recurrent bouts of arthritis. Repeated attacks over many years is common and more than 40 percent of the patients end up with chronic and disabling arthritis, heart disease, or impaired vision. [722]

## Nursing Experience

My friend contracted Chlamydia from her sexually active husband who was engaging in sex with others. She was among the 85% of women who had no symptoms. Suddenly, she began to experience pain and swelling of her knees, ankles, and elbows resulting in hospitalization. She became crippled and could not walk. The doctors had to insert large needles into her joints to remove the fluid. Upon laboratory examination, they found Chlamydia was causing this rare form of very painful arthritis. There is no known cure for this and she will have to live with Reiter's Syndrome (Reactive Arthritis) for the rest of her life.

## New research links Chlamydia to Autism

Autism is a neurodevelopmental disorder which manifests itself in abnormal social interaction, communication ability, patterns of interests, and patterns of behavior. **AUTISM** has become more well-known in today's society. As a school nurse, I am even more aware of the increased incidence rate of the school children whom I serve. Autism research continues to be conducted in several major universities. In one study, blood samples were drawn from autistic children. Chlamydia and other infectious agent's antibodies were noted. The researchers hypothesize these germs are crossing the placenta's blood-brain barrier and affecting the brain of the fetus during the pregnancy. Autistic children have varying degrees of learning disabilities and social issues. [8]

## Chlamydia causes blindness in newborns

Chlamydia causes **trachoma** Trachoma is a chronic eye infection (follicular conjunctivitis) that leads to scarring in the conjunctiva and cornea. The World Health Organization (WHO) estimates that approximately *six million cases of blindness* are due to trachoma in the world each year. If it is not diagnosed and correctly treated, it can produce cornea damage known as *trichiasis.* The WHO estimates that there are eleven

million cases of *trichiasis* each year in the world. [27]

## Nursing Experience

Nearly every newborn baby is treated for potential eye

infections immediately after birth (due to Chlamydia and

Gonorrhea) by applying an antibiotic eye ointment to both eyes.

Every baby I have assisted in delivering received antibiotic

ointment to both eyes immediately following birth. Rarely, a

mother would refuse the treatment for her newborn.

### Chlamydia Cases in California

| | | |
|---|---|---|
| 2000 | 95,392 | cases |
| 2001 | 101,944 | cases |
| 2002 | 110,288 | cases |
| 2003 | 117,428 | cases |
| 2004 | 122,197 | cases |

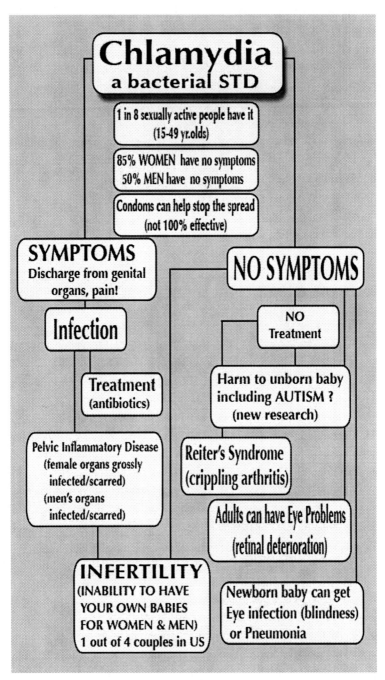

# Chlamydia
## a bacterial STD

1 in 8 sexually active people have it
(15-49 yr.olds)

85% WOMEN have no symptoms
50% MEN have no symptoms

Condoms can help stop the spread
(not 100% effective)

**SYMPTOMS**
Discharge from genital
organs, pain!

**NO SYMPTOMS**

Infection

NO
Treatment

Treatment
(antibiotics)

Harm to unborn baby
including AUTISM ?
(new research)

Pelvic Inflammatory Disease
(female organs grossly
infected/scarred)
(men's organs
infected/scarred)

Reiter's Syndrome
(crippling arthritis)

Adults can have Eye Problems
(retinal deterioration)

**INFERTILITY**
(INABILITY TO HAVE
YOUR OWN BABIES
FOR WOMEN & MEN)
1 out of 4 couples in US

Newborn baby can get
Eye infection (blindness)
or Pneumonia

# CHAPTER FIVE

## What is HPV (Human Papillomvirus)?

**How many people have HPV?**

> *1 out of 2 Sexually*
> *Active 15-49 Yr Olds*
> *HAVE HPV*

**At least 20 million Americans are already infected with HPV.** Dr. John Douglas (Director of the Division of STD Prevention at the CDC), recently estimated that *1 out of 2 sexually active Americans* (age 15-49 yr olds) will have HPV.[25] Cumulative prevalence rates are as high as 82% AMONG ADOLESCENTS IN SELECT POPULATIONS. [16, 32]

By age 50, at least 80 percent of women will have acquired genital HPV infection. About 6.2 million Americans get a new genital HPV infection each year.

Genital HPV infection is an STD caused by a group of viruses including more than 100 types. Thirty-five types are spread through sexual contact causing cervical cancer, genital

warts, and other genital cancers. [11]

## Genital Warts - Initial visits to physicians' offices: United States, 1966-2004

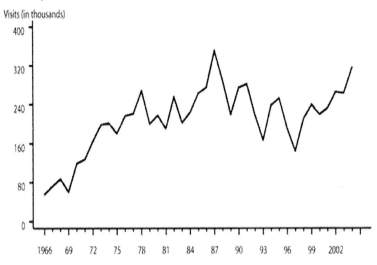

Note: See Appendix. The relative standard error for these estimates range from 40% to 60%. SOURCE: National Disease and Therapeutic Index (IMS Health)

---

### HPV causes Cancer
### in Women (cervix) and Men (Penis)

---

Many types of HPV are harmless and the healthy

human body can rid itself of the virus. Two of the types

(16&18) are known to cause cancer in women and more

recently in men.

The death rate in America from HPV (cervical cancer) was 3, 900 women in 2003 and estimated to be 3,705 for 2005. Worldwide the death rate is much higher from HPV. An annual pap screening for sexually active women is one confirmed way to help prevent cancer from developing in the cervix and has reduced death rates in the U.S. Pap screenings are recommended annually for women beginning at age 18 or whenever sexual activity begins.[29]

Once I understood the link between HPV and cervical cancer in women, I learned that men can also become infected with HPV leading to **cancer of the penis or anus.** Although penile and anal cancers are relatively rare at this time, it is important for men to understand that they can also get HPV leading to cancer.

**"The American Cancer Society estimates that about 1,530 new cases of penile cancer will be diagnosed and an estimated 280 men will die of penile cancer in 2006. Penile cancer occurs in about 1 in 100,000 in the United States." [34]**

"Genital HPV infections are transmitted through skin-to-skin contact, and because infections can occur in male and female genital areas that are not covered by a latex condom, condoms cannot offer complete protection from genital HPV infection," stated Dr. Douglass of the CDC in a Webcast, 2006. **Condoms do not stop the transmission of HPV** according to the CDC. [32,36,19,11,7]

## Nursing Experience with Cervical Cancer

One morning I received a phone call from a mother of four teenagers. Knowing of my women's health nursing background, she called requesting information about her 18 year old daughter. The family's medical group was urgently trying to reach her daughter with a pap screening result. I asked what the result was and she informed me that her daughter had a "4th stage" pap screening. A "4th stage" pap meant that this 18 year old girl had cervical cancer. Her daughter openly admitted that she engaged in early sexual activity beginning in the 9th grade and had continued with multiple partners throughout high school. *Both parents were surprised and unaware of their daughter's sexual activity throughout high school.*

The majority of early teen sexual experiences occur between the hours of three and six o'clock in the afternoon while parents are working and students are not chaperoned. In addition, research indicates that first teen sexual experiences occur with alcohol consumption. Parents can help prevent these situations by closely monitoring their students' activities and assuring adult supervision when necessary.

## HPV causes Genital Warts

**Genital warts** are caused from HPV (types 11 and 16). These warts appear on the genital area in males and females. If warts appear it is important to obtain treatment and have them removed. Various ways of removing warts include freezing, burning, surgical removal, and applying special medications to the affected area. If warts are not removed and treated, they can lead to cancer. **These warts have also been found in the**

**throats of adults.** Officials believe this could be the result of oral sex but it is not confirmed at this time. [11,17,19,28,29,32]

*HPV spreads from skin to skin including genitals to genitals, hand to genitals, mouth to genitals, etc. (HPV is not primarily spread through bodily fluids.) HPV spreads from skin-to-skin contact. <u>Condoms do not prevent the spread of HPV.</u>* [7]

## Nursing Experience with Genital Warts.

One afternoon while working in Labor and Delivery, I received report on a 17 year old female patient in active labor with a history of genital warts. Not thinking much about it, the doctor made rounds and wanted to examine her cervix to evaluate labor progress. When I assisted the doctor with the exam, I was not prepared for what I was about to see.

The genital warts were covering her perineum (genital area). I noticed at least thirty or more genital warts. Seeing the warts shocked me as though I had just seen a horror movie. The warts were cauliflower-like in appearance, in various shapes and sizes. The image of that 17 year old girl's case of genital warts has been forever embedded into my memory.

## Recurrent Respiratory Papillomatosis (RRP)

Women with HPV can transmit this virus to their unborn babies known as Recurrent Respiratory Papillomatosis (RRP). First-born children delivered vaginally to young mothers (under age 20) with active HPV condyloma during pregnancy are at greatest risk. The mechanism is not completely understood. Cesarean section deliveries do not always prevent transmission of the virus; it possibly crosses the placenta. [41]

When a baby is infected with the virus, warts can develop **in the child's throat**. JORRP (Juvenile Onset Recurrent Respiratory Papillomatosis) is almost always diagnosed by age ten and usually before age five. These warts are much more aggressive and fast growing than the warts which appear in adults. The warts which grow in children's throats require surgery. Some children require up to 150 surgical treatments in their lifetime. Some children require

tracheotomy performed (a hole in the throat area to assist with

breathing) due to so many surgeries to remove the warts.

## Genital Warts Can Be Transmitted to Your Babies

### Nursing Experience with RRP.

A nurse/friend who works part-time for a large Los

Angeles area medical center requested that I share the story of

her patient. Her patient, a 14 year old boy, had RRP (recurrent

respiratory papillomatosis). He recently had another surgery to

remove HPV warts from his throat. Due to all of the scar tissue

and damage from previous wart removal, his esophagus had to

be permanently closed and he had a gastrostomy tube (G-tube)

for feeding surgically inserted.

A G-tube is used for people who cannot eat with their mouths. It is a tube which goes through the abdomen directly into the stomach. This 14 year old boy will never be able to eat or drink by mouth again. Instead, he will have to feed himself through a tube which goes directly to his stomach. This young man had no choice; his mother's choices caused this irreversible condition.

According to the latest CDC treatment guidelines, condoms *may reduce the risk* of spreading HPV. <u>Research does not back up that claim</u>.

**PARENTAL POINTS TO MAKE WITH YOUR KIDS:**

1. Condoms do not stop HPV.
2. HPV causes cancer and warts in women and men.
3. HPV can be passes onto your babies causing lifelong problems.

**HPV Vaccine**

Most adults do not know what HPV is and most students I talk to have never heard of it. Recently, due to a new immunization which has been developed, HPV is gaining recognition. The HPV vaccine will help with four of the most common types of HPV which are known to cause cervical cancer and genital warts. The vaccine must be given prior to engaging in sexual activity to be effective. There is limited research available on the effectiveness of the vaccine at this time. However, the vaccine sells for $120. It is interesting that the public had never been informed about HPV until the drug companies had a vaccine for it.

"In June 2006, the ACIP (Advisory Committee on Immunization Practices) voted to recommend the first vaccine developed to prevent cervical cancer and other diseases in females caused by certain types of genital human papillomavirus (HPV). The vaccine, Gardasil, protects against four HPV types, which together cause 70% of cervical cancers and 90% of genital warts." (CDC)

"The Food and Drug Administration (FDA) recently licensed this vaccine for use in girls/women, ages 9-26 years. The vaccine is given through a series of three shots over a six month period." (CDC)

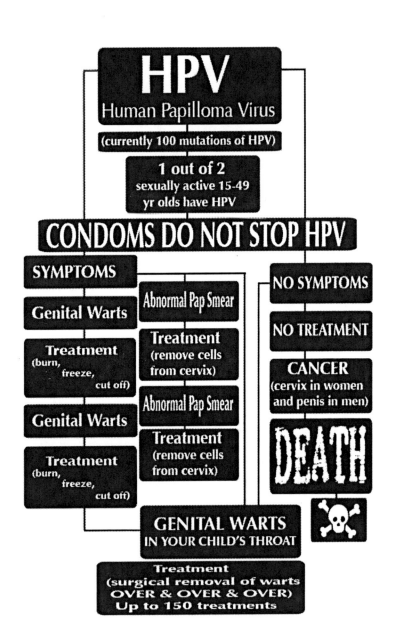

# CHAPTER SIX

## Gonorrhea

**Gonorrhea, a bacterial infectious disease, is the second most common reported bacterial STD in the U.S. and can be spread through contact with the penis, vagina, mouth, or anus.** Ejaculation does **not** have to occur for gonorrhea to be transmitted or acquired.11 Gonorrhea can also be spread from mother to baby during delivery. Any sexually active person can be infected with gonorrhea. In the U.S. the highest reported rates of infection are among *sexually active teenagers, young adults, and African Americans.*[7]

The **symptoms** in men include a burning sensation when urinating, or a white, yellow, or green discharge from the penis. Sometimes men get painful or swollen testicles. The symptoms in women are often mild, **but most women who are infected have no symptoms.** Even if symptoms are present they can be mistaken for a bladder or vaginal infection. Signs and symptoms in women include a painful or burning sensation when urinating, increased vaginal discharge, or vaginal bleeding between periods. [7]

In women, gonorrhea is a common cause of pelvic inflammatory disease (PID). About 1 million women each year in the U.S. develop PID. Women do not necessarily develop symptoms but if they have symptoms they can be very severe. Abscesses can form in the abdomen causing pain and fever. Long lasting chronic pelvic pain and abscesses in the abdomen can occur. Men can get epididymitis, a painful condition of the testicles which can lead to infertility (the inability to reproduce your own babies). Several antibiotics can successfully cure gonorrhea in teenagers and adults. [7,12,16]

Gonorrhea is caused by *Neisseria gonorrhea*, a bacterium that can grow and multiply easily in the warm, moist areas of the reproductive tract, including the cervix (opening to the womb), uterus (womb), and fallopian tubes (egg canals) in women, and in the urethra (urine canal) in women and men. [11] Latex condoms, when used consistently and correctly, *can reduce* the risk of transmission of gonorrhea. **The surest way to avoid transmission of gonorrhea is to abstain from sexual intercourse, or to be in a long-term mutually monogamous relationship with a partner who has been tested and is known to be uninfected.**[12]

CDC estimates that more than 700,000 persons in the U.S. get new gonorrheal infections each year. Gonorrhea: Disease Rate Falls to Historic Low **But Drug Resistant-Gonorrhea is on the Rise**. Gonorrhea is the second most commonly reported infectious disease in the United States, with 330,132 cases reported in 2004.

According to the CDC, *Gonorrhea, like Chlamydia, is substantially under diagnosed and under reported*, and approximately twice as many new infections are estimated to occur each year as are reported.[12] *The reported gonorrhea rate in the United States remains the highest of any industrialized country and is roughly 50 times that of Sweden and eight times that of Canada.*

## Nursing Experience #1 – Gonorrhea and the Pregnant Woman

While working in the Obstetrics and Gynecology Clinic, I had to telephone a patient who was 8 months pregnant to inform her that she had gonorrhea. Her husband had been SEXUALLY ACTIVE OUTSIDE OF THEIR MARRIAGE and brought home gonorrhea to his pregnant wife. This patient sobbed hysterically into the phone. I waited silently on the line and then instructed her to come immediately to the clinic for treatment. If treatment was complete, there would be less danger of her transferring Gonorrhea to her baby during her upcoming delivery.

## Nursing Experience #2 – Sixth Grade Students and Gonorrhea

More recently, working as a school nurse, I received a phone call from my elementary school principal. **The Public Health Department had just notified her that three of our 6**[th]

**grade students had gonorrhea**, one girl & two boys. Sadly, we had reported this girl to Child Protective Services (CPS) due to our suspicions of her being sexually molested. Evidently, she had been sexually molested and in turn she had sex with two 6$^{th}$ grade boys. All three were infected with gonorrhea.

# CHAPTER SEVEN

## Syphilis

Syphilis, a curable, bacterial STD, is often called "the

great imitator" due to the many signs and symptoms which are

indistinguishable from other diseases.[22] Syphilis passes from

person to person through direct contact with a syphilis lesion.

Lesions occur mainly on the genitals, lips, and in the mouth.

Transmission occurs during oral, anal, and/or vaginal sex. Most

transmission occurs between people *who are not aware* of their

infection.

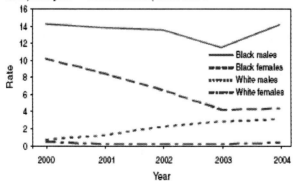

**FIGURE. Rates* of primary and secondary syphilis cases among non-Hispanic blacks and non-Hispanic whites, by sex, race, and year — United States, 2000–2004**

* Per 100,000 population.

**Syphilis is a systemic (widespread) infection that progresses if untreated through typical stages-primary, secondary, latent and tertiary (Medical Institute).** Usual symptoms of primary syphilis are a painless ulcer accompanied by lymph node enlargement; the ulcer heals without treatment. Secondary syphilis causes a flu-like illness accompanied by enlarged lymph nodes and a rash that may go unnoticed. Syphilis can cause corneal ulcers of the eyes leading to blindness. [24]

Symptoms are absent during latent syphilis. Tertiary syphilis can affect the nervous system (causing dementia), the cardiovascular system, and soft tissue or bone. Transmission from an infected mother to her infant can also occur during pregnancy and result in congenital syphilis. [16,17,28]

"Syphilis is highly infectious but easily curable in its early (primary and secondary) stages. *If untreated,* it can lead to serious long-term complications, including nerve, cardiovascular, and organ damage, and even death. Congenital syphilis can cause stillbirth, death soon after birth, and physical deformity and neurological complications in children who survive. Syphilis, like many other STDs, facilitates the spread of HIV, increasing transmission of the virus at least two- to five-fold".[29]

Reported cases of syphilis decreased from 1946-2000. Rates began to **increase** in 2001. Oral sex appears to have been an important mode of syphilis transmission in numerous recent outbreaks[17]

**Nursing Experience**

As a nurse manager, I was responsible for every aspect of my department. My unit was a Labor, Delivery, Postpartum, and Nursery Unit. We cared for our patients from their labor until discharge home of mother and baby. One morning, we had a full term healthy patient deliver a beautiful baby girl weighing 7 pounds 8 ounces. Immediately after delivery I noted a syphilis chanchroid on the baby's forehead.

As the nurse manager, I had to arrange for a helicopter transport to the nearest NICU. When a baby is born with secondary syphilis, a lesion on the outside of the baby most often indicates serious problems for the internal organs. Newborns infected with syphilis may suffer severe consequences _not completely relieved_ by treatment, including neurological damage and death. 28 Both parents denied having a history of syphilis. This beautiful baby girl's lesion came as a terrible surprise to everyone.

 **PARENTAL POINTS TO MAKE WITH YOUR KIDS:**

1. **Syphilis often has no symptoms.**
2. **Syphilis can be transferred to your baby causing very serious health problems.**
3. **Oral sex is transmitting Syphilis in today's culture.**

**As a nursing professor** this past semester of fall 2006, my students were assigned to the NICU of a large Orange

County teaching hospital. Each clinical day I would make my rounds on my twelve assigned student nurses. A female newborn baby was admitted to the NICU immediately following her birth with active syphilis. She was being tested to determine the severity of her infection. The nursing staff was extremely careful with this baby due to the fact that her syphilis infection could potentially infect others. The prognosis for this baby was poor and she was showing signs of a fatal condition.

# CHAPTER EIGHT

## Trichomoniasis...Eww!

Trichomoniasis (trich) is a microscopic parasite found

worldwide and is one of the most common sexually

transmitted diseases. Trich affects both men and women,

although, symptoms in women are more common than in men.

More than 8 million cases are reported each year.

**Figure 41. Trichomoniasis and other vaginal infections in women -
Initial visits to physicians' offices: United States, 1966-2004**

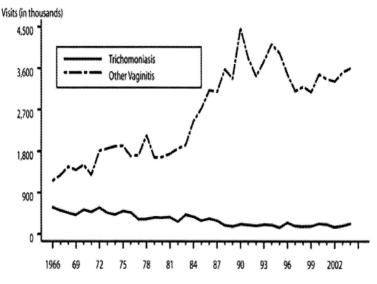

Note: The relative standard error for these estimates range from 16% to 30% and for other
vaginitis estimates range from 30% to 60%. SOURCE: National Disease and Therapeutic Index
(IMS Health)

At the 2006 STD Conference, a multi-city CDC study found that 1 in 7 patients were infected with Trich and it affects older women (age 34-39) more frequently. [29]

Trich is spread through sexual activity. A common misbelief is that infection can be spread by a toilet seat. This is unlikely because the parasite cannot live long in the environment or on objects. Trich is treatable with an antibiotic. Signs and symptoms range from having no symptoms to a foul smelling or frothy green vaginal discharge.

**Nursing Experience:**

On a personal note, every patient I have cared for in Labor & Delivery who had trichomonous, was easily identified by **the** *odor.* This infection produces the most nauseating, foul, strong odor forcing caregivers to breathe through their mouths to avoid using their sense of smell.

# CHAPTER NINE

## HIV/AIDS Continues to Spread

HIV (the human immunosuppressant virus) was identified in the early 1980s. This virus was first discovered in young homosexual males presenting with Kaposi's sarcoma and Pneumocysttis carini pneumonia. HIV continues to spread. **In 2004, there were 38,730 new cases in the US, a 10% increase, and 15,798 deaths which is a 10% increase.** *Known people living with AIDS are reported at 415,193.* **HIV has not gone away.** There are new medications on the market called antiretrovirals which help prolong the life of its victims. There is **no cure** for HIV/AIDS. [14]

In the United States, AIDS is the 5th leading cause of death in people 25-44 years of age. Cases of AIDS reported since 1981 are 753,907. The number of people who have died of AIDS in the U.S. is 438,795. Of the new cases of AIDS, 67% are men and 33% are women. Condoms are reportedly

85% effective in preventing the spread of AIDS. However, the research reports vary. Condom effectiveness varies from research report to research report.

## Nursing Experience #1

I cared for one patient with a known history of HIV who chose to conceive and give birth to three babies. Each baby was treated immediately after birth for the first six weeks of life with an antiviral medication. Due to the confidentiality issue I was unable to learn if these babies had converted to HIV (which means to become HIV positive). There was a 50% chance that each baby could have HIV which is the virus that causes AIDS.

## Nursing Experience #2

Another patient whom I cared for had a boyfriend in the final stages of AIDS at the time of their baby's birth. He was transported in to her Labor Room in a wheelchair due to his weakened state to sit at the bedside. Several hours later, a beautiful baby girl was born. The AIDS infected father sat crying, seeing his baby girl, knowing that his life was nearly over.

## Nursing Experience #3

This past year, working as a school nurse, I had a kindergarten student who had been born with HIV. No one knew he was HIV positive except for his teacher, the principal, and me. His health was progressively declining as the year went by. He would most likely not live to be 10 years old. This child never had a chance to choose for himself. Sadly, he was born infected with HIV due to his mother's choices.

## Nursing Experience #4

For my Master's Program Project, I taught 500 eighth grade science students about STDs in the classroom as their guest speaker. At the completion of my presentation I allowed ample time for questions. One 8th grade male student asked me about HIV, "Do some people live longer than others with AIDS?" I replied, "Yes, depending on time of diagnosis and treatment." I asked him why he had asked that question. This student explained to me and his classmates that his male cousin had began experimenting with sex at age thirteen. The cousin contracted HIV and died of AIDS at age 18. This student was shocked and saddened due to the early death of his cousin at such a young age.

---

**HIV IS SPREADING AMONG TEENS.**
USUALLY THERE ARE NO SYMPTOMS
FOR YEARS.
**HIV CAUSES AIDS & KILLS.**

---

# CHAPTER TEN

## Bacterial Vaginosus (BV) & Group B Strep

At the 2006 National STD Conference, researchers analyzed data from a health survey of nearly 2,000 women and found that 1 in 4 women have BV and 1 in 2 black women have BV.29 <u>BV (Bacterial Vaginosus)</u> and other STDs are estimated to cause *30 to 40 % of premature labors and births.*

*BV is the most common vaginal infection in women of childbearing age.* In the United States, as many as 16 percent of pregnant women have BV.

<u>Preterm birth and low birth weight are the leading causes of infant death and disability in the United States and there has been no reduction in more than 20 years.</u> It is estimated that 30 to 40 percent of excess preterm births and infant deaths are due to STDs and bacterial vaginosus. [13]

**"BV is not completely understood by scientists," according to the CDC. BV is associated with having a new sex partner or having multiple partners. It is seldom found**

**in women who have never had intercourse.  The basic prevention steps include (1) being abstinent, (2) limit the number of sex partners, (3) do not douche, and (4) use all of the medicine prescribed for treatment of BV, even if the signs and symptoms go away.** *I find it interesting that condoms are not recommended in any way.*

## Nursing Experience:

I have cared for hundreds of preterm patients throughout the 80s and 90s with infections affecting their pregnancy prior to the identification of BV.  Many patients lost their babies or their babies were born prematurely and often severely damaged from these infections.

**Group B Strep** (GBS) is a bacterium which is harmless to the mother ***but deadly to the newborn baby.***  Most women in California are screened for Group B Strep at the beginning of their pregnancy and at 36 weeks.  If the patient is positive, antibiotics are given through an intravenous line during labor to prevent the baby from becoming infected at birth. Researchers now feel that GBS is not sexually transmitted.

## Nursing Experience

Group B Strep nearly killed a newborn baby delivered at my unit in 1997. The newborn baby was discharged home approximately 12-24 hours after delivery which was the standard of care at that time. Both mother and baby were in good health and seemed perfectly fine.

**Forty-eight hours after discharge, his mother frantically returned with a bluish-colored, barely breathing newborn baby.** Immediately, the newborn was transported via helicopter to a large NICU. He was admitted and aggressively treated for 30 days with strong antibiotics, He miraculously survived the infection. I learned later from out chief physician that Group B Strep is deadly to newborns and can quickly kill.

**Some STDs, such as genital herpes and bacterial vaginosus, are quite common in pregnant women in the**

United States. Other STDs, notably HIV and syphilis, are much less common in pregnant women.

# CHAPTER ELEVEN

## Sexually Transmitted *EMOTIONAL ISSUES*

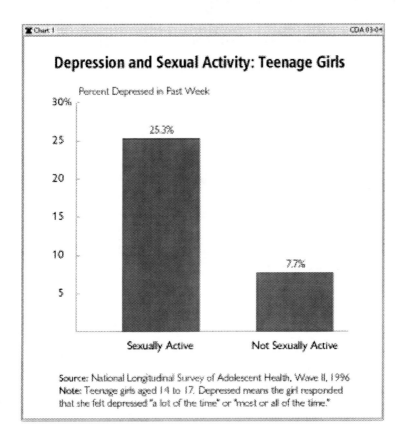

**Depression and Sexual Activity: Teenage Girls**

Percent Depressed in Past Week

- Sexually Active: 25.3%
- Not Sexually Active: 7.7%

Source: National Longitudinal Survey of Adolescent Health, Wave II, 1996
Note: Teenage girls aged 14 to 17. Depressed means the girl responded that she felt depressed "a lot of the time" or "most or all of the time."

A doctor of adolescent health, Dr. Meg Meeker, has stated that teenage sexual activity routinely leads to emotional turmoil and psychological distress. Sexual permissiveness leads to empty relationships, to feelings of self-contempt and worthlessness. All of these lead to *depression*. [17]

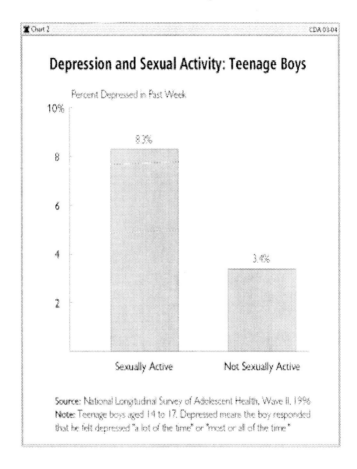

Teenage boys age 14-17 years were reportedly twice as depressed as their male friends who were not engaging in sexual activity.

## Depression and Sexual Activity

|  | Never/Rarely Depressed | Depressed Sometimes | Depressed A Lot | Depressed Most/ All of the Time |
|---|---|---|---|---|
| **BOYS 14-17** | | | | |
| Sexually Active | 63.3% | 28.4% | 5.0% | 3.3% |
| Not Sexually Active | 76.2% | 20.3% | 2.6% | 0.8% |
| | | | | |
| **GIRLS 14-17** | | | | |
| Sexually Active | 36.8% | 37.9% | 15.5% | 9.8% |
| Not Sexually Active | 60.2% | 32.1% | 4.9% | 2.8% |

Source: National Longitudinal Survey of Adolescent Health, Wave II, 1996

When you compare the numbers, it is obvious that sexual activity takes its toll on young women and men who are engaging in early sexual activity. Once again, abstinence until marriage is a good solution to prevent the emotional damage caused by early sex.

Parents agree that sexually active teens are more depressed than their peers who are not having sex. [35]

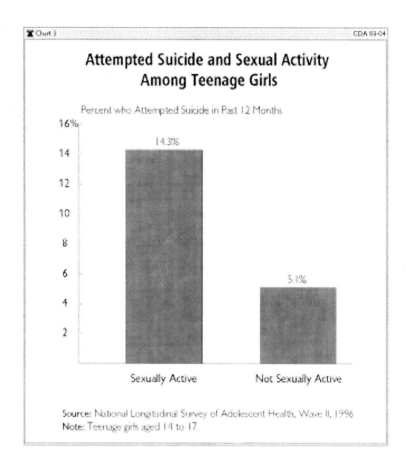

## Attempted Suicide and Sexual Activity Among Teenage Girls

Percent who Attempted Suicide in Past 12 Months

14.3%

5.1%

Sexually Active     Not Sexually Active

Source: National Longitudinal Survey of Adolescent Health, Wave II, 1996
Note: Teenage girls aged 14 to 17.

Another identified emotional issue connected to early

sexual activity is **attempted suicide.**(18) Fourteen percent of

sexually active teenage 14 to 17 year old girls reported

attempting suicide compared to 5.1% girls who are not sexually

active. [24]

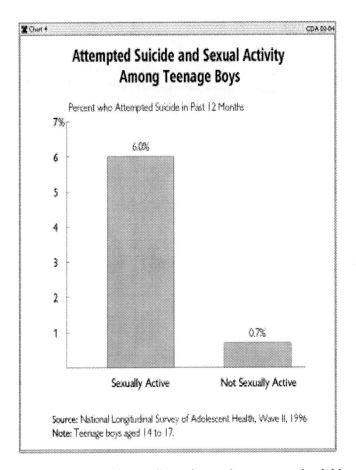

**Attempted Suicide and Sexual Activity Among Teenage Boys**

Percent who Attempted Suicide in Past 12 Months

6.0% — Sexually Active

0.7% — Not Sexually Active

Source: National Longitudinal Survey of Adolescent Health, Wave II, 1996
Note: Teenage boys aged 14 to 17.

Six percent of sexually active males attempted suicide compared to 0.7% of not sexually active 14 to 17 year old males. [24]

## Percentage Reporting Depression or Suicide Attempts, by Sexual Activity

|  | Male | Female |
|---|---|---|
| Sexually Active and Depressed | 8.30 | 25.31 |
| Standard Error (in Percentage Points) | (1.71) | (4.50) |
| Not Sexually Active and Depressed | 3.43 | 7.67 |
| Standard Error (in Percentage Points) | (0.74) | (0.95) |
| Sexually Active and Attempted Suicide | 6.00 | 14.26 |
| Standard Error (in Percentage Points) | (1.54) | (3.37) |
| Not Sexually Active and Attempted Suicide | 0.73 | 5.09 |
| Standard Error (in Percentage Points) | (0.31) | (0.84) |

Source: National Longitudinal Survey of Adolescent Health, Wave II, 1996

Three out of four girls **(72%) regret** having early sexual experiences. With teen boys 50% regret it and wish they would have avoided it. Unfortunately, young people engaging in sex are much less likely to be happy individuals. [23]

**Nursing Experience:**

As a labor and delivery nurse, I have cared for many 13 year olds through 17 year olds in labor. Unfortunately, I have never assisted with a teen delivery which was sincerely joyous. Amazing new life was being birthed but the circumstances usually seemed so sad. Often, parents would disown their daughter for being pregnant. Several times my young patient hid the pregnancy until she was in active labor.

I have had many opportunities to care for teens in labor due to my eagerness to accept the assignment. I love the next generation very much and I connect with them. When I would ask my teen patient why she chose to get pregnant, many times the response was, "I didn't think I could get pregnant having sex only once." The regrets were always obvious, not with words but with an underlying, overwhelming sense of responsibility.

Table 2                                CDA 03-04

# The Majority of Sexually Active Teens Wish They Had Waited Longer Before Beginning Sexual Activity

| Wish They Had Waited Longer Before Starting Sexual Activity | All Sexually Active Teens | Sexually Active Boys | Sexually Active Girls |
|---|---|---|---|
| Yes | 63% | 55% | 72% |
| No | 32% | 39% | 25% |

Source: National Campaign to Prevent Teen Pregnancy, June 2000.
Note: Survey covers sexually active teens aged 12 to 17.

**Girls who begin voluntary sexual activity at ages 13 or 14 will have, on average, more than 13 voluntary** non-marital partners during their lives. By contrast, women who began sexual activity in their early 20s will have, on average, 2.7 sexual partners during their lives. [23]

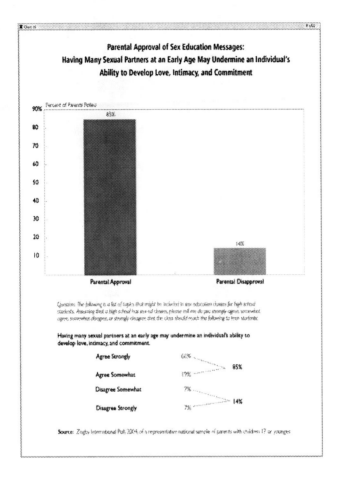

**Parental Approval of Sex Education Messages:**
**Having Many Sexual Partners at an Early Age May Undermine an Individual's**
**Ability to Develop Love, Intimacy, and Commitment**

Question: The following is a list of topics that might be included in sex education classes for high school students. Assuming that a high school has sex ed classes, please tell me do you strongly agree, somewhat agree, somewhat disagree, or strongly disagree that the class should teach the following to teen students:

Having many sexual partners at an early age may undermine an individual's ability to develop love, intimacy, and commitment.

| | | |
|---|---|---|
| Agree Strongly | 66% | 85% |
| Agree Somewhat | 19% | |
| Disagree Somewhat | 7% | 14% |
| Disagree Strongly | 7% | |

Source: Zogby International Poll, 2004, of a representative national sample of parents with children 17 or younger

# Early sexual activity seriously undermines the ability of girls *to form stable marriages* as adults.

When compared to women who began sexual activity in their twenties, girls who engaged in sexual activity at ages 13 or 14 were less than half as likely to be in stable marriages in their 30s. [23]

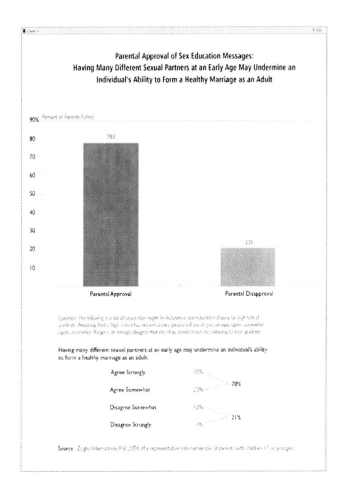

*Early sexual activity seriously undermines the ability of girls to form stable marriages as adults. When compared to women who began sexual activity in their twenties, girls who initiate sexual activity at ages 13 or 14 were less likely to be in*

*stable marriages in their thirties.  Beginning sexual activity at an older age, however, is linked to higher levels of personal happiness in adult years.* [23]

## Nursing Experience

For the past 18 years I have served time each week working with teenagers in a youth group environment.  My experience includes working as a Camp Nurse each year at Camp Cedar Crest in the mountains of Southern California.  As a Camp Nurse and weekly youth leader, I have observed depression first hand along with the feelings of emptiness and sadness when these teen relationships suddenly end.  I have consoled many young ladies and young men in their emotionally shattered states.

*Important Points to Remember:*

1. **Having early sex causes emotional damage including depression.**

2. **Waiting until later will help your student to succeed academically.**

3. **Engaging in early sex will NOT help your student in any way.**

4. **Abstinence until marriage helps keep healthy emotions.**

# CHAPTER TWELVE

## What Parents Should Do NOW!!!

Begin talking to your own teenagers and pre-teens about the serious consequences of early sexual activity. As a same sex parent, *you are the most influential person* in your child's life. Mothers talk to your daughters; fathers speak to your sons. Single parents talk to your children. Herpes and HPV are two viruses which condoms do not stop from spreading. Chlamydia and Gonorrhea usually have no symptoms. All of these STDs cause very serious consequences which will affect their lives forever.

*The number of teenagers engaging in oral sex has doubled in the past decade.* **Oral sex is spreading many STDs including syphilis, HIV, gonorrhea, Herpes, and HPV. Some of these organisms remain in the throat without symptoms spreading with each contact. In speaking to teens throughout the past few years, I have learned that many teenagers believe that oral sex does not spread STDs.** [17]

Educate your peers and encourage them to discuss sexual activity and the serious consequences with their teens. The consequences of STDs *will significantly alter* the future of our children. With recent research linking Chlamydia to Autism, the HPV virus being passed to the newborn, and Herpes killing newborns, why would any potential parent choose to take the risk?

**We must stop sugar coating the myth about condoms.** Preteens and teenagers must be equipped with *the truth* to help them make wise decisions about their future. Condoms have always been one of the *least effective* forms of birth control. **Condom use has increased among teens and sexual activity has declined yet the STD epidemic rages forward.** 34 According to the Youth Risk Behavior Survey (YRBS), from 1991-2003, condom use has increased from 46.2 % to 63% and sexual intercourse has decreased from 54.1% to 46.7%. Yet even with these improving numbers, STDs continue to soar.

Make sure your teens are supervised—unsupervised

teens have sex. Research says that most teen sex occurs

between three and six o'clock in the afternoon while parents

are working.

## National Youth Risk Behavior Survey: 1991-2003
## Trends in the Prevalence of sexual Behaviors

| 1993 | 1995 | 1997 | 1999 | 2001 | 2003 | Changes from 1991-2003 | Changes from 2001-2003 |
|---|---|---|---|---|---|---|---|
| **Ever Had Sexual Intercourse** | | | | | | | |
| 53.0 (+/-2.7) | 53.1 (+/-4.5) | 48.4 (+/- 3.1) | 49.9 (+/- 3.7) | 45.6 (+/- 2.3) | 46.7 (+/- 2.6) | Decreased 1991-2003 | No Change |
| **Had Four or More Sexual Partners During Lifetime** | | | | | | | |
| 18.7 (+/-2.0) | 17.8 (+/-2.7) | 16.0 (+/- 4.0) | 16.2 (+/- 2.6) | 14.2 (+/- 1.2) | 14.4 (+/- 2.0) | Decreased 1991-2003 | No Change |
| **Currently Sexually Active** (Had Sexual Intercourse During the 3 Months Preceding Survey) | | | | | | | |
| 37.5 (+/-2.1) | 37.9 (+/-3.5) | 34.8 (+/- 2.2) | 36.3 (+/- 3.5) | 33.4 (+/- 2.0) | 34.3 (+/- 1.0) | No Change 1991-2003 | No Change |
| **Condom Use During Last Sexual Intercourse** (Among Currently Sexually Active Students) | | | | | | | |
| 52.8 (+/-2.7) | 54.4 (+/-3.5) | 56.8 (+/- 1.6) | 58.0 (+/- 4.2) | 57.9 (+/- 2.2) | 63.0 (+/- 2.5) | Increased 1991-2003 | Increased |

What Is the National Youth Risk Behavior Survey

(YRBS)? The national YRBS monitors priority health risk

behaviors that contribute to the leading causes of death,

disability, and social problems among youth and adults in the

U.S. The national YRBS is conducted every two years during

the spring semester and provides data representative of 9th through 12<sup>th</sup> grade students in public and private schools throughout the United States." [34]

The evidence points to the fact that condoms are a *very poor form* of protection against these microorganisms. **The only 100% protection against STDs and their consequences is <u>delaying</u> <u>sexual</u> <u>activity</u>.**

*When 800 sexologists were asked if they met the person of their dreams and that person had HIV, how many of them would trust a condom for protection?*

 **Not <u>ONE</u> sexologist responded in favor of *trusting their own health* to a condom!!!**

If these professionals would not trust their health and well being to a condom, why are we as a nation promoting the use of condoms to our youth? [1]

<u>The single most important fact to convey to your teenagers is that many STDs have no symptoms.</u>

Students who are sexually active most likely have one or more STDs and are spreading them without knowing it. This epidemic continues to spread out of control with 15-19 year old females and 20-24 year old males leading the numbers of reported cases.

**Monitor what your teens and pre-teens see on television. Exposure to sex on television or films may encourage teens to initiate sexual activity.** (Rand)

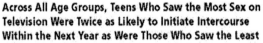

**Across All Age Groups, Teens Who Saw the Most Sex on Television Were Twice as Likely to Initiate Intercourse Within the Next Year as Were Those Who Saw the Least**

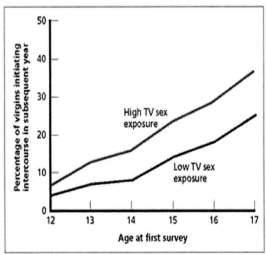

SOURCE: *Rand Health. Does Watching Sex on Television Influence Teens' Sexual Activity? Retrieved from www.rand.org/pubs/research*

*Since the 1970s, pornography has been poisoning the brains of America's youth. Aaron Hass, author of "Teenage Sexuality," surveyed* over six hundred males and females and found that almost all of the males and over ninety percent of the females had "looked at sexy books or magazines." Hass also found that 60 percent of the boys and over 40 percent of the females had seen a sexual movie. His conclusions were that most children believed the pornographic "information" they saw and engaged in copycat sex acts. Hass concluded that "Pornography provides teenagers with a sexual education." [39]

**The Rand Organization completed two studies; key findings included "(1) Teens who watch a lot of television with sexual content are more likely to initiate intercourse in the following year, (2) Television in which characters talk about sex affects teens just as much as television that actually shows sexual activity, (3) Shows that portray the risks of sex can help educate teens."**

**I ENCOURAGE PARENTS TO:**

1. **Educate and update your understanding of STDs.**
2. **Start discussing the short-term and long-term consequences of early sexual activity with your children.**
3. **Monitor what your teens/preteens are watching on television and on the internet.**

Parents, you can make a difference in your child's life by investing your time and discussing the consequences of engaging in early sexual activity.2 **It is time to expose the STD epidemic and talk about it.** Your child's health is the key to their future success. Research confirms that a parent or an interested adult can affect a teenager's choice to have sex by simply showing interest and discussing it. Your child's future depends on knowing all the facts and knowing that their parent cares about them enough to talk about sex.

Parents and all concerned adults armed with the *truth* could win the battle against the half-truths of our culture and reduce the devastating effects to our youth now and in the future. The impact on Public Health in America could potentially be altered in a positive way.

My goal in writing this book is to challenge every reader (parents, teens, and all concerned adults) with, *"What can you do to change the culture we live in and encourage our youth to value their health, their bodies, and their emotions?" Just as I have gathered information, coupled with my experience and written this book,* **I believe every person can take an active part on this issue.** Let's change history together and fight for the health and future of our teens!

# CHAPTER THIRTEEN

## My Master's Project:
## Do Students Learn the STD Facts Better from an
## Expert Nurse or Their Science Teacher?

### Abstract

Research has revealed that teens generally do not perceive themselves as at risk for acquiring HIV, HPV, and other STDs (Butts, 2002). Successful primary prevention interventions include teaching risk reduction skills with education, making a personal pledge to oneself, parental involvement in discussing sex, and feeling that parents or adults care. Interventions must be made at multiple levels to educate and equip adolescents, parents, and teachers with the tools to make healthy, safe choices. This program plan was designed to intervene at these levels and ultimately help reduce the numbers of new cases of STD/STIs among adolescents and encourage parental annual pap screenings. After completing the education intervention, data supports the positive impact of the Advanced Practice

Nurse in educating students of the short and long-term consequences of STDs.

# An STD Prevention Education Intervention for 8th Grade Science Students

## Program Plan

Sexually transmitted disease and infection (STD/STI) rates are highest among 15 to 19 year old females and 20 to 24 year old males in the United States (healthypeople.gov). Despite the burdens, costs, complications, and preventable nature of sexually transmitted diseases, they remain a significant public health problem. The estimated annual costs of adolescent STDs are 9.3-15.5 billion dollars (guttmacher.org 2004). When compared to other industrialized nations, the United States has failed to go far enough or fast enough in its national attempt to contain acute STDs and STD-related complications. STD rates in this Nation exceed those in all other countries of the industrialized world including the countries of western and

northern Europe, Canada, Japan, and Australia
(healthypeople.gov)

In generating the Effect Theory, the determinant factors which have led to this epidemic health problem include early onset of sexual activity, lack of protection, multiple sexual partners and lack of education (Issel, 2004). The antecedent factors include age, culture, and ethnicity. This population is 75.5% Hispanic and within this Hispanic population the majority of parents have an elementary school education or no formal education. The contributing factors to be considered include cultural practices to marry young, failure to complete high school, and encouragement to join the work force to generate income as soon as possible. The interventions to educate students, parents, and community could potentially impact the health outcomes by decreasing the high numbers of cases of adolescent STD/STIs. The short term and long term consequences of STD/STIs could be decreased by these educational strategies and the monetary expense of treating these conditions could be reduced substantially.

## Community Assessment

A community assessment was conducted for the City of Ontario with a focus on Vina Danks Middle School. The findings included modest incomes and low educational levels with 61% of the adult population having a high school education or less (city-data, 2005). The median age is 27.6 years, largest group 0-9 year olds (20%), and 75% Hispanic population (Husing, 2004).

The literature review concluded that Hispanic women are dying twice the rate of other ethnicities due to invasive cervical cancer caused by Human Papillomavirus (MMWR, 2002). Condoms do not stop the transmission of HPV. The rate of Herpes is one in four women and one in five men of the 15 to 49 year old age groups and condoms do not stop the transmission of this virus (CDC, 2005). Chlamydia is reportable to the CDC due to its major cause of infertility. Chlamydia rates are one in eight; however, 85% of women and 50% of men are asymptomatic. These three STDs became the subject of my primary prevention education intervention program

## Community Diagnosis

The community diagnosis with highest priority was lack of knowledge of HPV among eighth grade adolescent females related to increasingly high numbers of STDs as demonstrated by pre self assessment surveys completed during Science class indicating a knowledge deficit. The highest second priority was lack of knowledge of HPV and pap screening among Hispanic women related to communication barriers, low education levels, and low socioeconomic status demonstrated by comparison between Hispanic women ands non-Hispanic women mortality rates (MMWR, 2002).

## The Vision

In conjunction with Healthy People 2010, the Vision of this plan is to have a community united in the promoting of adolescents being free from debilitating and life-altering consequences of sexually transmitted diseases and infections. Adolescents have a higher degree of susceptibility than do older women because the ectropian of the cervix of a female teenager is more likely to become infected than that of a woman in her twenties (NAID, 2002). Researchers have estimated that a sexually active fifteen year old has a one in eight chance of developing pelvic inflammatory disease (PID), but by age twenty-four the probability has decreased to one in eighty (Anderson, 1998). By introducing the short term and long term consequences of STDs, students will be equipped and encouraged to make healthy choices for their future and to avoid sexual experiences until later in life.

## The Mission

The Mission of this program is to reduce high-risk sexual behavior that leads to STDs and to teach behavior modification skills to 8th grade adolescent science students. This program will target social and psychological skills that is necessary to avoid high-risk behaviors such as early sexual activity. This program will operate on the premise that adolescents who delay sexual activity will have high educational aspirations, peers with similar norms, and parent-child relationships characterized by supervision, support, and open communication (aafp.org)

## The Objectives

The first objective is to postpone sexual intercourse until after high school. The second objective is to encourage sexually active students to become responsible, to learn the importance of obtaining early treatment, and consistent follow-up for any STD/STI. The third objective is to reduce disease exposure by advising individuals at risk to avoid sexual contact with persons who have a high probability of being infected.

## The Strategy

This program is working toward the effective delivery of HIV/STD prevention education within the context of coordinated school health education in the classroom. An emphasis has been placed on the short term and long term consequences of STD/STIs. The first level of education has been directed toward adolescents within an 8th grade science class. This lesson was provided within the reproductive system unit.

A parent seminar was also offered at Vina Danks Middle School for an after school session for all parents. The attendance was minimal with only 25 parents attending. Unfortunately, the immigration issue became politically intense in the U.S. during the time of this intervention adversely affecting the turn-out of parents. An interpreter was provided for Spanish speaking parents.

A peer group of selected science students was additionally trained to provide personal contact and follow-up support. The peer group meetings were successful as the interest for the topic grew and students became empowered to speak to their peers regarding this sensitive topic.

## The Action Plan

The Action Plan included a pre and post self evaluation survey given before and after the presentation. The presentation was provided by an expert in the field of STD/STIs. The pre survey served as a discussion tool during the lesson. The post survey served as an indicator as to how many of the key points were retained. During the presentations three *Tree of Impact* charts focusing on Herpes, Chlamydia, and HPV were utilized as the major teaching tools (Lowenstein, 2004). These Tree of

Impact charts for Herpes, Chlamydia, and HPV visualized the prevalence rates, symptoms, long and short-term consequences and condom efficiency/inefficiency for each STD. A control group at another school site provided comparison data. Eighth grade science students completed a pre self evaluation survey prior to their coordinated school health education unit on HIV/STDs. Following the unit control site students completed a post self evaluation survey. These quizzes were administered to students by their classroom teachers.

**Inclusion and Exclusion Criteria**

The inclusion criteria for this sample included literacy. Each student must have been able to read English at no less than a 5th grade level. Each student must have been able to write and respond to true, false, or I don not know questions. Students were both male and female and have attended public school for the previous four years. Each student must have been enrolled in a middle school science class at Vina Danks Middle School or Oaks Middle School.

The exclusion criteria included eighth grade students who are not literate. Students who are emotionally disturbed or non-English speaking were excluded from this study.

## Important Variables

The important variables measured were knowledge of HPV and the consequences of HPV including cancer and genital warts. The knowledge of Herpes, prevalence, and consequences was measured. The knowledge of Chlamydia including the consequences and asymptomatic nature of the infection was measured. The knowledge of choices made during the teen years and their impact on their future was measured.

## Statistical Data

A comparison was made of the post surveys between the intervention site and the control site. The null hypothesis was the there would be no difference between the survey scores. The hypothesis was that there would be a significant difference between the control site and the intervention site scores. Chi Square analysis was used and found to be significant. The number was 164. The degrees of freedom (df) was 123. Chi squared was 88.95 and the $p$ value was .00895. I rejected the null hypothesis with a=.01 level of significance. All assumptions for Chi-squared test were met.

## Goal

The goal for this program is to increase awareness, knowledge, risks, and consequences of STD/STIs including HIV among eighth grade science students and their parents. This goal was met with regards to students as demonstrated by the post survey data.

## Post Self Assessment Survey

In accumulating the data, the intervention site and control site answers were divided into male or female responses. In the following ten survey questions, the first percentage will indicate the male response and the second percentage will indicate the female response rate with a slash (/) separating the two response rates.

**In Question One,** "Condoms do not prevent the spread of HPV or Herpes," the intervention site answered correctly 84/86% compared to the control answering 57/55% correctly.

**In Question Two,** "HIV is transmitted through oral, anal, and vaginal sex," the control site exceeded the intervention site by17/20%. This question was added to assess the education provided by public education science standards due to mandated HIV education in California.

**In Question Three,** "HPV is a virus that causes genital warts and cancer," the intervention site scored correctly 88/94% compared to the control site answering 46/50% correctly.

**In Question Four,** "HPV can be transferred to the unborn baby causing warts in the child's throats," the intervention site answered 85/91% correctly compared to 64/76% at the control site.

**In Question Five,** "More women die from cervical cancer (caused by HPV) than AIDS each year," the intervention sample correctly answered 78/72% compared to the control site 38/42% correctly.

**In Question Six,** "Chlamydia is a bacterial infection," the intervention site answered 84/82% correctly compared to the control site answering 66/64% correctly.

**In Question Seven,** "Chlamydia infection often has no symptoms," the intervention site answered 58/64% correct compared to the control site answering 44/46%. These low scores indicate a need for me to change my presentation to more clearly communicate the asymptomatic nature of this bacterium.

**In Question Eight,** "Herpes can kill a newborn baby," the intervention site scored 95/98% correctly compared to the control site with 43/35% answering correctly. My actual nursing experience included sharing the loss of a healthy newborn just seven days after birth.

**In Question Nine,** "STDs can be transferred to the unborn baby without the mother knowing she has anything wrong with her," the intervention site answered 88/95% correctly compared to the control site answering 78/80% correctly.

**In Question Ten**, "My choice to have sex as a teenager will affect my future," both the intervention and control site females answered 86/84%. The males answered from the control answered 70% correctly compared to intervention site 86%.

## Objectives

By June 2006, 90% of eighth grade science students at Vina Danks Middle School will have received STD/STI consequence based sex education by an expert at Vina Danks Middle School as evidenced by completion of pre and post self evaluation quizzes. This objective was met by May 2006.

By June 2006, 80% of parents of eighth grade science students of Vina Danks Middle School will have received STD/STI consequence-based education by attending parent seminar as evidenced by sign-in sheet for parental seminar (Porsche, 2004). Unfortunately, this goal was not met due to the intense immigration issue which surfaced politically in our nation at this time May, 2006. Only 10% of parents attended the seminar and due to the various year end activities the principal was unable to schedule another seminar on the impacted school calendar.

## Funding

Funding for this project was provided by Ontario-Montclair School District. As a credentialed employee of the district I utilized the copy machines and paper available for the surveys. My out-of-pocket expense was $165.00 to have professional Tree of Impact Charts made by professionals. Due to this being my project, my time was free to the district which would have otherwise cost an estimated $3,000 for the 22 classroom presentations covering 10 working days.

## Conclusion

In conclusion, Healthy People 2010 contains grand resolutions similar to this program's mission which is to help individuals of all ages to increase life expectancy, improve quality of life, and to eliminate health disparities among different segments of the population. This program has proven to be statistically significant in providing evidence-based research data to students in the classroom by an Advance Practice Nurse. My future plan is to continue this intervention strategy into the next school year and provide additional education to the adults in the community at large. Several teachers requested that I reproduce the Tree of Impact Boards so that they could be displayed in the classroom. As multilevel education strategies are tried in this plan, we can only hope that individuals will make wiser choices in the future as they are empowered to take ownership of their health.

## Final Comments

My Master's Project had a surprising result. I proved my hypothesis. I had always felt that when you hear information from someone knowledgeable and experienced the information could go much deeper in to the listeners' hearts and minds. The majority of science teachers who I worked with had a passion to teach the students this important life-altering STD information. However, the students learned much more from me, the nurse expert.

**I am not sure what the perfect solution is to this raging epidemic but I do know we need change. We must do everything we can to inform them of the truth as concerned adults.**

Appendix A.

Selected STDs and complications - Initial visits physicians'
offices: United States, 1966-2004

| Year | Genital Herpes | Genital Warts | Vaginal Trichom- oniasis* | Other Vaginitis* |
|---|---|---|---|---|
| 1966 | 19,000 | 56,000 | 579,000 | 1,155,000 |
| 1967 | 15,000 | 72,000 | 515,000 | 1,277,000 |
| 1968 | 16,000 | 87,000 | 463,000 | 1,460,000 |
| 1969 | 15,000 | 61,000 | 421,000 | 1,390,000 |
| 1970 | 17,000 | 119,000 | 529,000 | 1,500,000 |
| 1971 | 49,000 | 128,000 | 484,000 | 1,281,000 |
| 1972 | 26,000 | 165,000 | 574,000 | 1,810,000 |
| 1973 | 51,000 | 198,000 | 466,000 | 1,858,000 |
| 1974 | 75,000 | 202,000 | 427,000 | 1,907,000 |
| 1975 | 36,000 | 181,000 | 500,000 | 1,919,000 |
| 1976 | 57,000 | 217,000 | 473,000 | 1,690,000 |
| 1977 | 116,000 | 221,000 | 324,000 | 1,713,000 |
| 1978 | 76,000 | 269,000 | 329,000 | 2,149,000 |
| 1979 | 83,000 | 200,000 | 363,000 | 1,662,000 |
| 1980 | 57,000 | 218,000 | 358,000 | 1,670,000 |
| 1981 | 133,000 | 191,000 | 369,000 | 1,742,000 |
| 1982 | 134,000 | 256,000 | 268,000 | 1,859,000 |
| 1983 | 106,000 | 203,000 | 424,000 | 1,932,000 |
| 1984 | 157,000 | 224,000 | 381,000 | 2,450,000 |
| 1985 | 124,000 | 263,000 | 291,000 | 2,728,000 |
| 1986 | 136,000 | 275,000 | 338,000 | 3,118,000 |
| 1987 | 102,000 | 351,000 | 293,000 | 3,087,000 |
| 1988 | 163,000 | 290,000 | 191,000 | 3,583,000 |
| 1989 | 148,000 | 220,000 | 165,000 | 3,374,000 |
| 1990 | 172,000 | 275,000 | 213,000 | 4,474,000 |
| 1991 | 235,000 | 282,000 | 198,000 | 3,822,000 |
| 1992 | 139,000 | 218,000 | 182,000 | 3,428,000 |
| 1993 | 172,000 | 167,000 | 207,000 | 3,755,000 |
| 1994 | 142,000 | 239,000 | 199,000 | 4,123,000 |
| 1995 | 160,000 | 253,000 | 141,000 | 3,927,000 |
| 1996 | 208,000 | 191,000 | 245,000 | 3,472,000 |
| 1997 | 176,000 | 145,000 | 176,000 | 3,100,000 |
| 1998 | 188,000 | 211,000 | 164,000 | 3,200,000 |
| 1999 | 224,000 | 240,000 | 171,000 | 3,077,000 |
| 2000 | 179,000 | 220,000 | 222,000 | 3,470,000 |
| 2001 | 157,000 | 233,000 | 210,000 | 3,365,000 |
| 2002 | 216,000 | 266,000 | 150,000 | 3,315,000 |
| 2003 | 203,000 | 264,000 | 179,000 | 3,516,000 |
| 2004 | 269,000 | 316,000 | 221,000 | 3,602,000 |

*Women only
SOURCE: National Disease and Therapeutic Index (IMS Health).
Retrieved from www.cdc.gov

# References

1. Anderson, Kerby. (1998).School-Based Health Clinics and Sex Education. Retrieved February 29, 2004 from http://www.probe.org.

2. Blake, S. M., Simkin, L., Ledsky, R., Perkins, C., & Calabrese, J. M. (2001, Mar-Apr). Effects of a parent-child communication intervention on young adolescents' risk for early onset of sexual intercourse. *Family Planning Perspective,* 33, 52-61. Retrieved March 5, 2005, from http://www.intapp.medscape.com/px/medlineapp/getdoc

3. Butts, J. B. & Hartman, S. (2002). Project BART: Effectiveness of a behavioral intervention to reduce HIV risk in adolescents. *The American Journal of Maternal/Child Nursing,* 27(3), 163-169. Retrieved April 29, 2005 from: http://nursingcenter.com/library/journalarticleprint.asp

4. Card, J. (1999). Teen Pregnancy: Do Any Programs Work? *Annual Review Public Health* 20:257-85.

5. Carter, T. (2003). Uganda leads by example on AIDS. *The Washington Times.* Retrieved 2/29/04 from www.washingtontimes.com/world/20030313.

6. Chesson, H.W., Blandford, J.M., Gift, T.L., Tao, G., & Irwin, K.L. The estimated direct medical cost of sexually transmitted diseases among American youth, 2000. *Perspectives on Sexual and Reproductive Health.* 36, 1. January/February 2004. Retrieved June 1, 2006 from http://www.guttmacher.org/pubs/journals/3601104.html

7. Chlamydia, gonorrhea, and HPV. National Institute of Allergy and Infectious Diseases. (2002). Retrieved on November 10, 2005 from http://www.naid.nih.gov.

8.  Cooper, E. L. (2003). Neuroimmunology of autism: a multifaceted hypothesis. *International Journal of Immunopathology and Pharmacology*, 16, 3, 289-292.

9. Corneal Ulcers. Health A to Z, Your Family Site. Retrieved July 9, 2006 from www.healthAtoZyourfamilysite.com

10. Genital Herpes, NIAID Fact Sheet. October, 2005. National Institute of Allergy and Infectious Diseases. US Department of Health and Human Services. Retrieved July 9, 2006 from http://www.niaid.nih.gov/factsheets/stdherp.htm

11.  Genital HPV Infection. CDC Fact Sheet. Retrieved August 2, 2006 from http://www.cdc.gov

12.  Gonorrhea. CDC Fact Sheet. Retrieved July 27, 2006 from http://www.cdc.gov

13.  Infertility treatment costs. Huntington Reproductive Center Medical Group. Retrieved July 19, 2006 from http://www.havingbabies.com/clinical -studies.html

14.  John Hopkins University, (2002, July 11).Zambia's HEART Program Evaluation Shows Youth Respond Positively to AIDS Prevention Plan Promoting Abstinence. Retrieved 3/3/04 from http://www.jhuccp.org/pressroom/2002/07-11.shtml

15.  Manhart, L.E. & Koutsky, L.A. (2002). Do condoms prevent genital HPV infection, external genital warts, or cervical neoplasia?: a meta-analysis. *Journal of the American Sexually Transmitted Diseases Association*, 29, 11. Retrieved December 11, 2005 from http://www.stdjournal.com/pt/re/std/fulltext.

16.  Medical Institute for Sexual Health. (2001). The Sexually Transmitted Disease Epidemic. Retrieved February 8, 2004 from www.w-cpc.org/sexuality/std.html.

17.  Medical Institute for Sexual Health (2003). Medically Speaking, Oral Sex and STDs. Sexual Health Update. Spring 2003. Retrieved June 7, 2006 from http://www.w-cpc.org/sexuality/std.html

18.  Meeker, Meg. Epidemic: How Teen Sex is Killing Our Kids. Washington D.C.: Regnery Publishing Company, 2002. p.12

19.  Moscicki, A. (2005). Impact of HPV infection in adolescent populations. *Journal of Adolescent Health*, 37, 6. Retrieved from http://www.jahonline.org/article

20.  Nells, J. (2003).Poll Shows Parents Support Abstinence-Based Sex Education. Retrieved February 29, 2004 from http://www.family.org

21.  RRP Foundation. Who Gets RRP? Retrieved July 16, 2006 from http:// www.rrpf.org/whatisRRP.html

22.  Rand Health. *Does Watching Sex on Television Influence Teens' Sexual Activity?* Retrieved from www.rand.org/pubs/research

23.  Reactive Arthritis (Reiter's Syndrome). Retrieved August 2, 2006 from http://en.wikipedia.org/wiki/Reiter's_syndrome

24.  Rector, R.E., Johnson PhD, K.A., Noyes, L.R., & Martin, S. *The Harmful Effects of Early Sexual Activity and Multiple Sexual Partners among Women: A Book of Charts.* The

Heritage Foundation. June 26, 2003. Retrieved May 3, 2006 from http://www.heritage.org/Research/Family/cda0304.cfm

25. Rector, R.E., Johnson, K.A., and Noyes, L.R. Sexually active teenagers are more likely to be depressed and to attempt suicide. Center for Data Analysis Report #03-04. June 3, 2003. Retrieved May 3, 2006 from http://www.heritage.org/Research/Family/cda0304.cfm

26. Stammers, T.G. (2003) Abstinence Under Fire. *Post Medical Journal*.79:365-6.

27. Subcommittee on Criminal Justice, Drug Policy and Human Resources. (February 12, 2004). Rep. Souder asks FDA for action on condom & HPV Information Law. Retrieved February 29, 2004 from http://www.abstinence.net/library/index.php?entryid=827

28. Trachoma. Division of Bacterial and Mycotic Diseases. Centers for Disease Control and Prevention. Retrieved July 9, 2006 from http://www.cdc.gov/ncidod/dbmd/diseaseinfo/trachoma

29. Tracking the hidden epidemics 2000, trends in STDs in the United States. National Center for HIV, STD, and TB Prevention. Retrieved May 17, 2006 from http://www.cdc.gov/nchstp/od/news/RevBrochure1pdffhaq.htm

30. Trends in Reportable Sexually Transmitted Diseases in the United States, 2003, 2004. National Data on Chlamydia, Gonorrhea, and Syphilis. CDC. Retrieved July 19, 2006 from http://www.cdc.gov/stds

31. Weinstock, H., Berman, S., and Cates, Jr., W. Sexually transmitted diseases among American youth: incidence and prevalence estimates, 2000. *Perspectives on Sexual and Reproductive Health*. 36, 1. January/February, 2004. Retrieved May 7, 2006 from http://www.guttmacher.org/pubs/journals/3601104.html

32. Weis, L. & Carbonell-Medina, D. (2000). Learning to speak out in an abstinence based sex education group: gender and race work in an urban magnet school. (Electronic Version). *Teachers College Network*, 102:620-630.

33. Webcast: Human Papillomavirus (HPV) and Cervical Cancer: An Update on Prevention Strategies Script. August 9, 2005. Director of CDC, Dr. Julie Gerberding, Dr. John Douglas, Director of Division of Sexually Transmitted Disease Prevention of the National Center for HIV, STD, & TB Prevention at CDC. Retrieved from http://www.cdc.gov/std/hpv

34. Wetzstein, C. Study links teen sex to depression, suicide. *The Washington Times: Nation/Politics.* 2003. Retrieved May 4, 2006 from http://www.washingtontimes.com/national/20030603-115719-1821r.htm.

35. What Are the Key Statistics About Penile Cancer? American Cancer Society. Retrieved from http://www.cancer.org

36. Youth Risk Behavior Surveillance, 2003. Retrieved May 23, 2006 from http://www.cdc.gov/mmwr/preview/mmwrhtml

37 Zogby International 2003 Survey on Parental Opinions of Character-Based, Abstinence-Until-Marriage Sex Education vs. Comprehensive ("Abstinence-First," Then Condoms) Sex Education. *Coalition for Adolescent Sexual Health.* Retrieved January 21, 2004 from http://.www.whatparentsthink.com

38. 2006 National STD Prevention Conference. Media Release Day 3. Retrieved July 16, 2006 from http://www.cdc.gov/stdconference/2006/media/day3.htm

39. Rand Health. Does Watching Sex on Television Influence Teens' Sexual Activity? Retrieved from http://www.rand.org/pubs/research

40. Hass, Aaron. *Teenage Sexuality.* New York: Macmillan, 1979.

41. Yliskoski, M., Puranen, N., Saarikoski, S., Syrjanen, K., and Syrjanen, S. Exposure of an infant to cervical human papillomavirus infection of the mother is common. *American Journal of Obstetrics & Gynecology.* 176, 5. 1039-1045. May 1997.

# DVD available in Summer 2007

Contact for free information regarding speaking engagements. Please call, write or e-mail the author at:

Becky Ettinger
19744 Beach Blvd. #248
Huntington Beach, CA 92648
(714) 536-3353 home
(714) 564-6868 office
E-mail: mimebeck@aol.com or ettinger_becky@sac.edu

(Please complete, detach and mail Order Form to the above address.)

## ORDER FORM – The Secret STD Epidemic

DVD Copy - $12.00 ea. (.PDF format)
Paperback Copy - $9.00ea.
DVD and/or Paperback Copy Orders of 10+ receive 10% Discount

| No. of Paperbacks | No. of DVDs | Total Quantity |
|---|---|---|
|  |  |  |

| | |
|---|---|
| Sub-Total | $ |
| Applied 10% Discount on Orders of 10+ | $ |
| Shipping & Handling Fees of $ .95 per book | $ |
| **Total Enclosed:** | **$** |

Please send me the number of books I have indicated. I have enclosed a check, money order or cashier's check, plus the $.95 per copy to cover postage and handling fees.* I understand that cash cannot be accepted as a form of payment.
My shipping information is as follows: (Please print)

| | |
|---|---|
| Name: | |
| Address: | |
| City: | State: | Zip: |
| Contact Phone: (Optional) | |

*Bulk orders may be subject to reduced shipping and handling rates dependent upon quantity and destination. Please call to confirm accurate pricing.
Please allow 4-6 weeks for delivery – For large, custom or rush orders, please call.

# Cover Photo

The couple pictured on the front cover is Brad Ettinger, Pro Surfer and model and Danielle (Hurley) Ettinger, model, teacher, and wife.

Brad and Danielle dated for 4 years from age 18 until age 22.

They made a commitment to remain abstinent until marriage.

In November of 2006 they were married. Their commitment to abstinence until marriage has been an example to their friends and professional colleagues.

Their hope is for the next generation to be wise and to follow their example.

It is worth the wait.

Printed in the United States
106668LV00002B/331-498/A